FOR DR. JONATHAN PASCOE IN HONOR OF HIS MEDICAL CONTRIBUTIONS TO THE U.S. AND NEW ZEALAND ANTARCTIC PROGRAMS — S.M.

ACKNOWLEDGMENTS

The author would like to thank the following people for sharing their expertise: Dr. Beau Riffenburgh, editor of *Polar Record* at the Scott Polar Research Institute, Cambridge, England; and Baden Norris, emeritus curator of Canterbury Museum, Christchurch, New Zealand. A special thank-you to the U.S. National Science Foundation for sending the author twice on expeditions to Antarctica. As always, a special thank-you to Skip Jeffery for his help and support throughout the creative process.

Text © 2008 by Sandra Markle.
Illustrations © 2008 by Phil.
All rights reserved.

Typeset in Old Claude and Vogue.
The illustrations in this book were rendered in acrylic on wood panel.

Manufactured in China.

10 9 8 7 6 5 4 3 2 1

Chronicle Books LLC
680 Second Street
San Francisco, California 94107

www.chroniclekids.com

Image Credits:
Page 12: © Hulton-Deutsch Collection/CORBIS; pages 13, 19, 30, 31 (bottom), and 32: licensed with permission of the Scott Polar Research Institute, University of Cambridge; pages 14, 17, 31 (top), and 39: courtesy of The Royal Geographical Society; page 37: courtesy of the author.

Library of Congress Cataloging-in-Publication Data
Markle, Sandra.
Animals Robert Scott saw : an adventure in Antarctica / by Sandra Markle.
p. cm.
ISBN: 978-0-8118-4918-0
1. Scott, Robert Falcon, 1868–1912—Juvenile literature.
2. Explorers—Great Britain—Biography—Juvenile literature. 3. Antarctica—Discovery and exploration—Juvenile literature. 4. Animals—Antarctica—Juvenile literature. I. Title.
G875.S35M27 2008
919.8'904—dc22
[B]
2006020920

ANIMALS *Robert Scott* SAW

An Adventure in Antarctica
by Sandra Markle

chronicle books · san francisco

NOTE TO PARENTS AND TEACHERS

The books in the Explorers series take young readers back in time to share explorations that had a major impact on people's view of the world. Kids will investigate why and how the explorers made their journeys and learn about animals they discovered along the way. They'll find out how some animals affected the outcome of the journey, helping explorers find their way, causing key events to happen, or helping the explorers survive. Young readers will also learn that, because of the explorers' journeys, animals were introduced to places they'd never lived before, sometimes with dramatic results.

The Explorers Series helps students develop the following key concepts:

From the National Council for the Social Studies:
Human beings seek to understand their historical roots and to locate themselves in time. Such understanding involves knowing what things were like in the past and how things change and develop. Students also learn to draw on their knowledge of history to make informed choices and decisions in the present.

From the National Academy of Sciences:
Making sense of the way organisms live in their environments will develop an understanding of the diversity of life and how all living organisms depend on the living and nonliving environment for survival.

CONTENTS

THE LAST FRONTIER

Imagine a place that is so far away from where most people live that for ages no one knew it existed. It can be reached only during the summer because in the winter it's surrounded by ice and it's dark nearly all the time. Much of the land is also covered in ice year-round, and the weather is among the fiercest in the world. This place is Antarctica (ant-ARK-ti-kuh).

Since it's such a long journey to get to Antarctica and conditions there are so unpleasant, why did Robert Falcon Scott go there twice? You may be surprised to learn that animals had a lot to do with why he went and also played a major role in what happened while Scott was there.

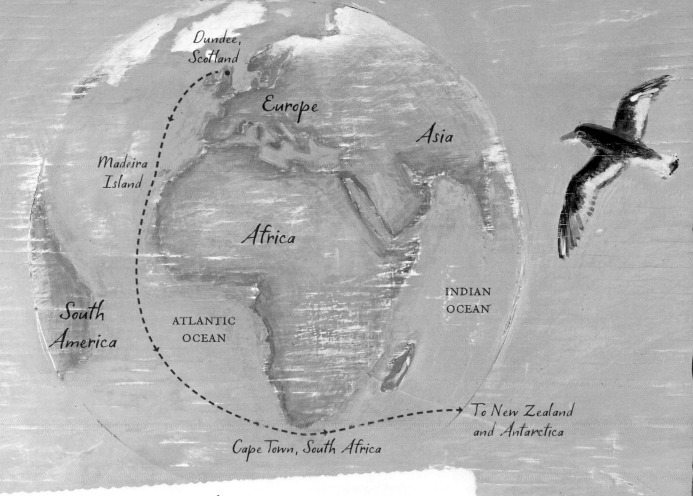

Dundee, Scotland

Europe

Asia

Madeira Island

Africa

South America

ATLANTIC OCEAN

INDIAN OCEAN

To New Zealand and Antarctica

Cape Town, South Africa

The Coldest Place on Earth

Once they arrived in Antarctica from Dundee, Scotland, Robert Scott's crew had to endure the coldest, driest, windiest continent on Earth. All but 2 percent of the land is covered in ice, and tiny insects and worms are the only creatures able to survive on land year-round.

Other Antarctic Facts:

- The coldest temperature ever recorded on Earth was -128.6 °F (-89.2 °C) in the interior of Antarctica.
- Antarctica has 70 percent of Earth's freshwater frozen as ice, and more than 90 percent of Earth's ice.
- If Antarctica's ice sheets melted, all of Earth's oceans would rise by 200–210 feet (60 to 65 meters).

TO THE ENDS OF THE EARTH

The 1890s through 1914 (when World War I began) were years when countries competed to be the first to explore the earth's frontiers. Two unexplored frontiers of special interest were the North Pole, in the Arctic (ARK-tik), and the South Pole, in the Antarctic. People lived in countries around the Arctic Circle, so explorers had some idea about the conditions of the North Pole. But reaching the South Pole meant crossing frozen land that no one knew anything about. Only whale and seal hunters had been anywhere near Antarctica, but they had not ventured inland. South Pole explorers were heading into the unknown.

Why Hunt Whales and Seals?

In the 1800s, whale oil for lamps was in great demand. Lightweight, bendable whalebone was used to make women's clothing, such as hoop skirts, which were fashionable at the time. Seals were hunted for their fur. Years of hunting had greatly decreased the numbers of whales and seals in much of the world, so hunters had to search for them in more remote places—even as far away as Antarctica.

AN EXPLORER'S BEGINNINGS

Born in 1868, Robert Falcon Scott grew up in a time when explorers were heroes and people were just beginning to explore Antarctica. In 1821, John Davis, a seal hunter from New Haven, Connecticut, made the first recorded landing in Antarctica, but it was not widely publicized. In 1895, while hunting for whales with Leonard Kristensen, Carsten Borchgrevink (KAR-stun bork-GRAY-vingk) claimed to be the first person to set foot on the Antarctic continent. In 1899, Borchgrevink returned with an expedition headed by Henryk Bull and funded by a British newspaper owner. For the first time, a team went to Antarctica just for the sake of exploration.

Robert Scott during his service as a naval commander

When Scott was 18 and a midshipman in the Royal Navy, he met Sir Clements Markham (MAR-kum), a noted geographer and president of the British Royal Geographical Society. Sir Clements was impressed with Scott's intelligence and enthusiasm—so much so that he followed Scott's progress in the navy with interest.

Several years later, Sir Clements arranged an expedition to Antarctica. He had a ship for the journey—the *Discovery*—but he needed a leader for the expedition. He chose the now 32-year-old naval commander Robert Falcon Scott.

Ross Sea, South Victoria Land, 1910.

Emperor Penguins
April. 17. 1902.

Capturing Wildlife

Dr. Edward A. Wilson was hired as the assistant surgeon for the Discovery expedition. But he was also a skilled painter and loved studying birds. He would be most remembered for dying with Scott. However, he is also remembered for his studies and paintings of Antarctica's wildlife, especially penguins.

PREPARATIONS

While Scott oversaw preparations for the expedition in England, other preparations were being made in New Zealand, where the ship would take on supplies before heading to Antarctica. The expedition's dogs were shipped to New Zealand ahead of the *Discovery*'s arrival. The dogs were put through training exercises to prepare them for pulling the sledges that would be used to carry heavy loads of supplies. The *Discovery* left Scotland on July 31, 1901. On board were all the supplies needed for the trip — scientific instruments, sledges, tents, fuel, cold-weather gear, and enough food to feed the expedition's 47 men for two years — and Scott's Aberdeen terrier.

Scott's terrier, Scamp

On the way to New Zealand, Scott stopped to investigate the wildlife on Macquarie (meh-KWAR-ee) Island, about 1,000 miles (1,700 kilometers) southeast of Australia. There, he and his crew saw penguins for the first time. They found a nesting colony of king penguins, a species second in size only to the emperor penguins they would later see in Antarctica. Scamp, unable to decide whether to run away from the penguins or chase them, did both.

SOUTH WITH THE BIRDS

On November 29, 1901, the *Discovery* sailed into Lyttelton Harbor in New Zealand. For almost a month, the crew overhauled the ship, loaded on more coal and supplies, and took on the sled dogs. Fearing life in Antarctica might be too hard for Scamp, Scott found a family in New Zealand to adopt him. Finally, on December 21, 1901, with an escort of five steamers loaded with cheering passengers, the *Discovery* sailed for Antarctica.

By the beginning of January 1902, the men of the *Discovery* expedition knew they were approaching Antarctica. They began to see birds they had not seen in warmer waters. They saw southern fulmars (FUL-merz), Antarctic petrels (PE-truhlz), and snow petrels. Dr. Wilson was especially impressed with the birds and spent hours on deck in the cold making sketches. Later, below deck, where it was warmer, he turned his sketches into lifelike watercolor paintings.

The *Discovery* surrounded by ice

On January 8, 1902, Scott and his crew saw Antarctica's frozen coast for the first time. The *Discovery* landed at Cape Adare, where Borchgrevink's party had wintered. When they set sail again, the *Discovery* was quickly surrounded by pack ice and had to push its way through.

SEAL STEAKS AND PENGUIN STEWS

By the end of January, the surface of the sea was freezing over. Scott anchored the *Discovery* in McMurdo Sound, where tall mountains blocked the strong winds blowing across the land. The men set up camp by assembling *Discovery* Hut, the precut hut they'd brought along.

As the weather grew colder, the men dressed in layers of clothes. They wore wool underwear and a couple of pairs of thick wool socks. Over these they wore trousers, shirts, sweaters, and, finally, coats. Their mittens were wolfskin lined with sheepskin, and their boots were reindeer hide with the fur inside. When they had to camp out, they slept in reindeer-hide pajamas inside reindeer-hide sleeping bags.

Why Reindeer Hide?

Reindeer hide is valued for its fur covering. Adapted to living in cold Arctic regions, reindeer have an extremely dense fur coat. There may be as many as 5,000 long outer hairs and 13,000 woolly underhairs per square inch (6 square centimeters). These hairs trap body heat and keep cold air from penetrating the fur.

SUMMER OF FIRSTS

On November 2, 1902, Scott, Dr. Wilson, and Ernest Shackleton headed south. Having 19 dogs pull their supply sledges made traveling easier, but it also caused problems. Instead of the usual dog biscuits, Scott brought dried fish. Unfortunately, the fish had spoiled when the *Discovery* sailed through the hot tropics on the way to Antarctica. The dogs refused to eat this food and grew weak. One by one they died. The few that survived were too weak to work, and the men had to haul the heavy sledges themselves.

Ernest Shackleton

Captain Scott

Dr. Wilson

A Warm Coat

Dried fish weren't the only thing that made life rough for the dogs of the Discovery expedition. They were from the Arctic region, where the seasons are the opposite of the seasons in Antarctica. When it's summer in the Arctic, it's winter in the Antarctic. Dogs usually shed their coats in the summer, when the weather gets warm. Still on the Arctic cycle, Scott's dogs started to shed just as the Antarctic weather became severely cold. Fortunately, after a couple of weeks, the dogs' bodies responded to the conditions and rapidly grew back their thick, woolly undercoats.

Brownie

The men became very attached to the dogs they worked with. Scott was especially fond of Brownie, a sled dog with a particularly gentle nature. Sometimes Scott allowed Brownie to sleep inside his tent while the other dogs slept outside in the snow. Scott was very sad when Brownie died.

The going was rough. There were blizzards. All three men suffered from scurvy, a disease that makes people weak and causes their joints to swell and their gums to bleed easily. Wilson also suffered from snow blindness, a temporary condition caused by sunlight reflecting off ice and snow. Finally, running out of food and energy, the group turned back a few days after Christmas. They had not reached the South Pole, but they had traveled farther south than anyone had before.

Daddy Duty

After mating, female emperor penguins each lay one egg in May or early June, during the Antarctic winter. Having used up a lot of energy to produce the egg, the female then heads for the sea to feed. The male balances the egg on its feet and covers it with a fold of skin on its belly. That way, the egg is kept warm for three to four months while the chick inside develops.

ANOTHER ICE YEAR

When Scott returned to McMurdo Sound in early February 1903, he discovered a relief ship, the *Morning*, in the harbor. The arrival of the ship should have meant the end of Scott's expedition; the *Morning* was supposed to accompany the *Discovery* back to New Zealand. However, the *Discovery* was trapped in the ice and couldn't sail. For a month both ships' crews worked to free the *Discovery*, but with little success. Finally, the *Morning* headed back to England, taking along a few of Scott's team and leaving behind fresh supplies and a few members of its crew as replacements. Scott was happy to remain in Antarctica. Now he could make further explorations the following summer.

Skuas hold the record for flying farther south than any other bird in the world.

Scott set his men to work preparing for the coming winter. He sent out hunting parties to kill seals and birds for meat. Dr. Wilson continued to sketch and paint. Unlike many artists of his day who produced portraits of animals that looked as though they were stuffed specimens, Wilson showed animals in action. This way, he shared all he observed: Antarctic birds in flight, seals nursing young on the ice, and emperor penguins raising their chicks. Hodgson also continued to catch and study sea creatures from under the ice.

Emperor Chicks

An emperor chick has fluffy down feathers, so it can't swim and hunt for food. It has to wait onshore for its parents to bring home food in their stomachs. Because getting to the sea and finding food takes time, the chick is likely to have a long wait between meals. But once a parent returns, the meal it brings up from its stomach can be equal to as much as a third of the chick's body weight.

When the winter was over and the sun finally returned, it was time for Scott to take a trip west up the Ferrar Glacier toward the Polar Plateau. This time, there were no dogs. The men would have to pull the sledges themselves.

While preparations for the expedition were being made, Dr. Wilson traveled to the emperor penguin rookery. He expected to see adults incubating eggs, but was shocked to see there were already large chicks. Until then, no one had guessed that any bird could hatch its eggs during the Antarctic winter.

On October 12, 1903, Scott and a support crew set out. It was not an easy trip. Strong winds forced them to stay in their tents for a few days, and the runners on the sledges needed repair. When they got underway again, one of the men hurt his back. With each problem, Scott sent another group of men back to the ship. Finally, on November 22, 1903, Scott continued with just two other men: Edgar Evans and William Lashly. When their food supply began to run out, Scott and the others were also forced to turn back.

HOME

Scott was ready to go home. He ordered his men to make every effort to saw a passageway through the ice for the ship. But he also sent out hunters to collect food—just in case. This time, the men discovered an Adélie penguin rookery with newly laid eggs, which they brought back for an egg feast.

In early January 1904, the *Morning* returned along with another ship, the *Terra Nova*. Working together, the crews of the three ships freed the *Discovery*.

Leopard Seals
Second only to the orca as Antarctica's top predator, the leopard seal is the largest kind of seal living year-round in Antarctica. Females grow larger than males, weighing over 900 pounds (408 kilograms) and measuring as much as 13 feet (4 meters) in length. They are fierce hunters and fast swimmers as they chase down and catch penguins and other seals.

By September 1904, Scott had returned to England. To his surprise, he was famous. People wanted to meet the man who held the record for traveling farther south than anyone had before. They were eager to hear about Antarctic wildlife: the penguins and other birds, the orcas, and the seals. The public also flocked to an exhibition of Dr. Wilson's lifelike paintings of Antarctic wildlife.

Scott continued to serve in the Royal Navy. After a while, he married and had a son. He began to think of going back to Antarctica, but the British government's interest in Antarctica had faded. He was not able to get anyone to fund another expedition.

BACK TO ANTARCTICA

In 1909, Ernest Shackleton, who had once been part of Scott's crew, returned from his own expedition to Antarctica. He didn't make it to the South Pole, but public attention around the world suddenly focused once again on the race to the South Pole. With this increased interest, Scott was able to fund a second Antarctic expedition.

On June 15, 1910, Scott and his crew set sail from England aboard the *Terra Nova*. They once again stopped in New Zealand, where they picked up supplies, sled dogs, and Manchurian-bred ponies trained for hauling heavy sledges. Scott's second expedition left for Antarctica on November 29, 1910.

Because Norwegian explorer Roald Amundsen was also headed for Antarctica, newspapers around the world reported that the two men were in competition to be the first to the South Pole. But Scott claimed that the primary focus of the *Terra Nova* expedition was to study Antarctica's rocks, weather, and wildlife. In fact, the original plan for the expedition was to set up camp at Cape Crozier so Dr. Wilson could study emperor penguins throughout the winter. Unfortunately, when the *Terra Nova* arrived at Cape Crozier, a wall of pack ice made it impossible for the crew to reach the shore. The *Terra Nova* sailed on to Cape Evans in McMurdo Sound and anchored there on January 4, 1911.

The Terra Nova stuck in the ice

Sea Creatures

As part of the expedition, Denis Lillie, the Terra Nova's biologist, collected many marine animals. He caught large shrimp, lots of fish, starfish, and Antarctic isopods, cousins of crayfish. Lillie was especially interested in the many sponges he discovered. Some, like the Antarctic red sponge, were brightly colored. Another kind, known as glass sponges, had silica, glasslike bits that helped give their bodies shape and strength.

Denis Lillie and one of his many sponges

Schoolchildren donated money to buy 33 Siberian dogs and 19 Manchurian ponies for Scott's expedition.

Manchurian Ponies

Scott chose these small, strong ponies to pull the sledges because they could pull more weight than the dogs could. The ponies were used to cold climates, but none as extreme as Antarctica's.

This is what each man ate each day of their sledging trip: meat (for stew), sugar, vitamin cookies, butter, cocoa, and tea.

Scott and his men soon set off with dog and pony teams. The plan was to deposit supplies along the route they would take to the South Pole the following summer. On the way, though, they faced many obstacles. Unusually warm weather made the snow soft, and the ponies pulling the heavy supply sledges sank deep into the snow. Scott sent some of his men back to the hut at Cape Evans for snowshoes for the ponies, and the ponies labored on. Then a blizzard struck, forcing the men to stay in their tents for three days. Finally, the supplies were deposited and it was time to head home. But the hard times weren't over yet.

The trip back to Cape Evans was toughest on the animals. Some of the ponies died in a blizzard. Others drowned after sea ice they were crossing broke up. When one of the dog teams ran onto a snow bridge—a patch of frozen snow that hides a deep crack in the ice—the bridge broke, and eight dogs dangled over a cliff by the ropes that hooked them to the sledge. Two fell out of their harnesses to a ledge below. The crew hauled the dogs still attached to the sledge to safety. Scott was lowered on a rope and rescued the dogs on the ledge.

Pony Snowshoes

The supplies for Scott's expedition included special snowshoes for its ponies. Looking like round tennis rackets, these were strapped to the pony's hooves. Just like human snowshoes, they spread the pony's weight over an area larger than its foot. That kept the pony from sinking deep into the soft snow and made walking easier.

How Emperors Stay Warm

Under their double layer of tightly packed feathers and skin, emperor penguins have a layer of blubber to keep them warm. To prevent heat loss through their feet while sitting on the ice, they rock backward and rest on their heels. They use their tail feathers, which have no blood flow and lose no heat, to prop themselves up.

IN SEARCH OF THE EMPERORS

In late June, Dr. Wilson and two other men, Apsley Cherry-Garrard and Henry "Birdie" Bowers, made a very dangerous journey to the emperor penguin nesting site at Cape Crozier. For 19 days they walked through the dark and freezing cold. Finally, they heard penguin calls and followed the sound to a cliff. The penguins were below, huddled on the ice-covered sea. With great effort, the men climbed down. They were the first people to see male emperor penguins incubating eggs.

Climbing back up the cliff, the men built an igloo of rocks and snow. They used their canvas tent for a roof. They planned to rest before starting back to Cape Evans, but a storm with hurricane-force winds ripped away their roof. The men burrowed into their sleeping bags to survive the freezing cold until the storm ended and they could head home.

Dogs and Ponies

Unlike dogs, ponies sweat. Fearing the ponies would freeze to death if put to work in extremely cold weather, Scott waited for temperatures to rise before he headed for the South Pole. This delay cost Scott precious time, causing many historians to wonder if Scott's team would have fared better if they'd used dogs, as Roald Amundsen's team did.

TO THE POLE

The sun rose and the days lengthened as Scott and his team made preparations for their trek to the South Pole. On November 1, 1911, with high hopes for success, Scott and 11 other men set out with sledges pulled by ponies and dogs. Four men with motor-powered sledges had already left. Scott hoped motor-powered sledges would save animals from working in such harsh conditions, but the sledges soon broke down and couldn't be fixed. The pony and dog teams struggled onward. One storm after another struck, with freezing cold winds and driving snow that piled up in deep drifts. One by one the ponies grew weak and died. By December 8, 1911, only the dogs and the men were left to haul the sledges.

When Scott reached the Beardmore Glacier (the largest in the world), he knew climbing it would be too much for the dogs. He ordered the dog teams to go back to *Discovery* Hut, built during Scott's *Discovery* expedition. The teams were to wait there until Scott and his team were scheduled to return. Then they would help Scott's weary team home.

Eight men went on pulling two sledges loaded with supplies. Finally, on January 4, 1912, Scott ordered three more men to head to *Discovery* Hut. He set off for the pole with the sledges and the remaining four men: Dr. Edward Wilson, Edgar Evans, Lawrence Oates, and Henry "Birdie" Bowers.

Discovery Hut

The three men heading to *Discovery* Hut thought their journey would be easy, but a blizzard held them up for three days. One of the men developed scurvy. The other two hauled him on the sledge until the effort became too much. One man stayed behind to care for his sick friend while the other went on for help. He met up with the dog-team drivers at *Discovery* Hut, and they rescued the two men who had stayed behind.

In early March the dog teams set out to meet Scott's team at an agreed-upon supply depot. They waited six days, but Scott's team never arrived. They finally decided Scott and the others must be dead and returned to Cape Evans to pass a very sad winter.

Dr. Edward Wilson   Robert Scott   Edgar Evans   Lawrence Oates   Henry Bowers

Scott's final expedition team

A WORLD CHANGED FOREVER

On November 12, 1912, the *Terra Nova* expedition's search party found the bodies of Robert Scott, Dr. Wilson, and Henry Bowers. They were inside their tent only 11 miles (17 kilometers) south of the depot where the dog teams had gone to meet them. The search party also found the men's diaries and letters. From these, they learned that the men had arrived at the South Pole on January 17, 1912, but not before Norwegian explorer Roald Amundsen had gotten there and planted the Norwegian flag. His team had beaten Scott's by 35 days.

Weak and disappointed, Scott and his men had started for home. In mid-February, Edgar Evans was the first to die from the cold, lack of food, and scurvy. The rest of the party went ahead, but only slowly. And the next month Oates, believing he was too weak to survive much longer, walked away into a storm. His death left more food for the others, but their rations finally ran out. When the cold became too much, Scott, Wilson, and Bowers also died. When the search party found the men, they said a prayer and left them in the snow.

On January 13, 1913, the remaining men and dogs of the *Terra Nova* expedition returned to New Zealand. The story of what had happened to Scott quickly spread around the world. Amundsen had earned the honor of being the first to reach the South Pole, but Robert Scott's effort to get there touched people's hearts. The courage shown by Scott and his team inspired others to explore remote parts of the world. However, it was not until 1956 that explorers returned to study the South Pole. Today, many scientists carry out investigations there. Some even live and work there year-round at the Amundsen-Scott South Pole Station.

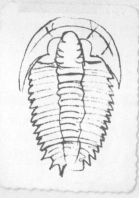

Final Discovery

The search party brought back the 35 pounds (16 kilograms) of rocks Scott's team had collected during their trek to the South Pole. The fossils in these rocks proved that 250 million years ago Antarctica was covered by forests. Years later, scientists would also discover fossils of plant-eating and meat-eating dinosaurs in Antarctica.

The route Scott chose to take up the west side of the Ross Ice Shelf had much worse weather than the eastern route Amundsen chose to take. This plus poor planning on Scott's part almost guaranteed Amundsen would reach the South Pole first.

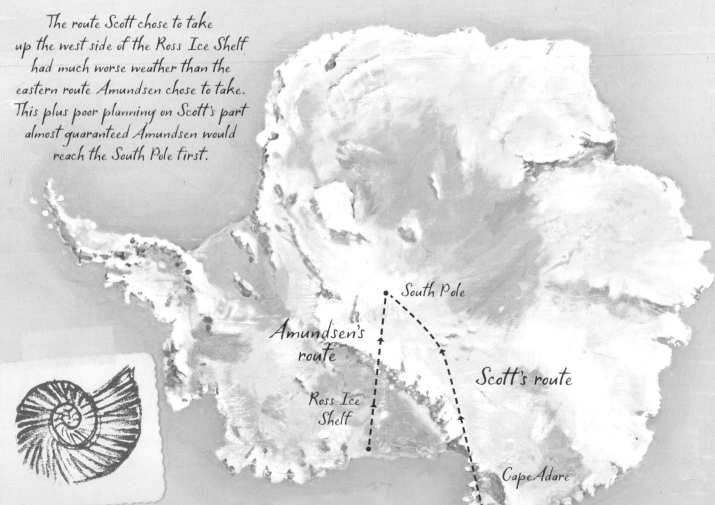

South Pole

Amundsen's route

Scott's route

Ross Ice Shelf

Cape Adare

GLOSSARY

Antarctica   the frozen continent at the southernmost part of Earth

blizzard   a storm with strong, cold winds blowing snow

crevasse   a deep crack in the ice

depot   a place where supplies are stored

expedition   a trip made for a special purpose

glacier   a large mass of ice that moves slowly downhill

pack ice   chunks of ice floating close together on the surface of the sea

rookery   a place where a group of birds gets together to mate and raise chicks

scurvy   a disease caused by a lack of vitamin C

sledge   a kind of long sled used for moving heavy loads across snow and ice

FOR MORE INFORMATION

To learn more about Antarctica and the exploration of this frozen continent, check out these books and websites.

Books:

Antarctica: The Blue Continent, by David McGonigal and Lynn Woodworth. Firefly Books, Ltd., 2003.
The photos alone make this book for older readers a virtual tour of this amazing place—one of the fiercest, most challenging environments on Earth.

Life under Ice, by Mary M. Cerullo and Bill Curtsinger (photographer). Tilbury House Publishers, 2005.
Dive under the ice in Antarctica with marine photographer Bill Curtsinger. Discover the wildlife at home in this extreme environment.

Pioneering Frozen Worlds: Polar Region Exploration, by Sandra Markle. Simon and Schuster, 1996.
See how both the Arctic and Antarctic regions have become laboratories for scientific research.

Polar Explorers for Kids: Historic Expeditions to the Arctic and Antarctic with 21 Activities, by Maxine Snowden and Jeanne Hanson. Chicago Review Press, 2003.
This book tells of famous expeditions to both poles and includes hands-on activities, such as a recipe for pemmican, a cold-weather survival food, and instructions for building a model igloo.

Super Cool Science: South Pole Stations, Past, Present, and Future, by Sandra Markle. Walker, 1998.
Explore the stations designed to help scientists explore the remote site Robert Falcon Scott struggled so hard to reach.

Web sites

South-Pole. Com http://www.south-pole.com/
Discover photos and information about Scott and other South Pole explorers and expeditions.

Virtual Antarctica http://www.doc.ic.ac.uk/%7Ekpt/terraquest/va/
Take a virtual trip to Antarctica. Through maps and amazing photographs you'll learn about the history of Antarctic exploration, current scientific investigations, conservation issues, and lots more.

U.S. South Pole Station http://www.nsf.gov/news/special_reports/livingsouthpole/index.jsp
Learn about the history of Antarctica and take a virtual tour.

INDEX